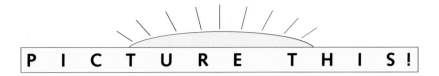

Summer

Karen Bryant-Mole

RIGBY
INTERACTIVE
LIBRARY

This edition ©1997 Reed Educational & Professional Publishing
Published by Rigby Interactive Library,
an imprint of Reed Educational & Professional Publishing,
500 Coventry Lane
Crystal Lake, IL 60014

Printed in China
01 00 99 98 97
10 9 8 7 6 5 4 3 2 1

Library of Congress Cataloging-in-Publication Data
Bryant-Mole, Karen.
  Summer / Karen Bryant-Mole.
    p.   cm. — (Picture this!)   Includes index.
  Summary: Text and labeled photographs identify things associated with summer.
    ISBN 1-57572-056-6 (lib. bdg.)
    1. Summer—Juvenile literature. [1. Summer.] I. Title.
    II. Series: Bryant-Mole, Karen. Picture this!
QB637.6.B79   1997
508.2—dc21   97-393
                                                            CIP
                                                            AC

Text designed by Jean Wheeler

Acknowledgments
The publisher would like to thank the following for permission to reproduce photographs:
Cephas, p. 15.(left); Nigel Blythe, James Davis, p. 14 (right); Eye Ubiquitous, p. 11 (left); Ken Oldroyd/Hutchison, p.15 (right); Christine Pemberton/Tony Stone Images, p. 6; John Edwards, p. 7 (left); Simon Jauncey, p. 7 (right); Raymond Gendreau, p.10 (right); Jerry Alexander, p. 11 (right); Mervyn Rees, p. 14 (right); Nabeel Turner, p. 18 (right); David Sutherland, p. 19 (left); Bob Thomas, p. 11 (right); Kevin Cullimore, p. 22 (left); Matthew McVay, p. 22 (right); Ulli Seer, Arthur Tilley, p. 23 (left); Adrian Murrel, p. 23 (right); Zefa, p. 10 (left), p. 18 (right).

Note to the Reader
Some words in this book may be new to you.
You may look them up in the glossary on page 24.

Contents

Fruit

These summer fruits are sweet and juicy.

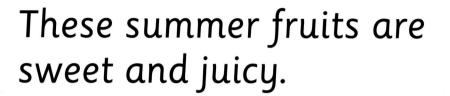

peaches

nectarine

melon

strawberries

On a Farm

There are lots of jobs to do on a farm in summer.

hay making

crop spraying

harvesting

watering

At the Beach

A day at the beach is fun
on a hot summer day.

sieve

rake

sea shells

sand pail

sand
shovel

9

Flowers

dahlia

poppies

lupines

Insects like
the bright colors.

**butterfly on
cosmos**

11

Salad

lettuce

tomatoes

cucumber

radishes

Together these
vegetables
make a
salad.

Holidays

Id ul-Adha in
Saudi Arabia

Independence Day
in the United States

Sanja Matsuri
in Japan

Dragon Boat festival
in Hong Kong

Clothes

Summer clothes help keep you cool.

**baseball
cap**

T-shirt

shorts

sandals

17

Keeping Cool

A summer's day can be very hot.

eating popsicles

drinking water

sitting in the shade

swimming

Picnic

It's fun to eat outside in warm weather.

What foods do you like to take on a picnic?

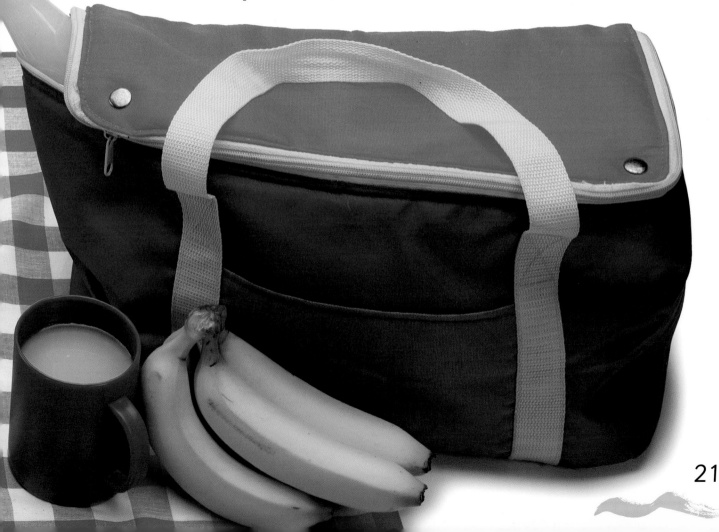

Sports

Outdoor sports
are fun to play
in summer.

swimming

tennis

beach volleyball

cricket

23

Glossary

cricket An outdoor game played by two teams, using a ball, bats, and wickets.

crop spraying Spraying crops to keep insects away.

Dragon Boat festival Chinese festival that remember the drowning of an ancient Chinese poet.

Id ul-Adha Festival during which followers of Islam share food with family and friends.

Sanja Matsuri Japanese festival held in May that celebrates hopes of a good harvest.

nectarine Fruit that looks like a peach.

Index